Boise State University Western Writers Series   Number 85

Edward Dorn

By William McPheron

Stanford University

Editors: Wayne Chatterton
James H. Maguire

Business Manager:
James Hadden

Cover Design by Arny Skov,
Copyright 1988

Boise State University, Boise, Idaho

Copyright 1988
by the
Boise State University Western Writers Series

ALL RIGHTS RESERVED

Library of Congress Card No. 87-73498

International Standard Book No. 0-88430-084-6

Quotations from Edward Dorn's poems by permission of the author.

Printed in the United States of America by
Boise State University Printing and Graphics Services
Boise, Idaho

Edward Dorn

Edward Dorn

Edward Dorn is a political poet committed to the ideals of democratic culture. A fierce partisan of the free play of critical thought, he is acutely sensitive to the socio-economic forces aligned against an open society. "Democracy," he insists, "literally has to be cracked on the head *all the time* to keep it in good condition" (*Contemporary Authors* 129), and he understands its most serious enemy to be capitalism's enormous power, which in the post-World War II era has reached beyond the marketplace to infiltrate and control every aspect of American life. Though he despises the bourgeois ethos that sustains these commercial interests, Dorn remains hostile to all parties and ideologies, rejecting liberal pieties as well as conservative platitudes. He advocates neither party nor platform but offers instead a tensely alert mind that challenges every form of political and cultural authority. The result is a series of imaginative, intellectually provocative, and steadily more disturbing images of the American nation.

The purpose of his art, as Dorn himself defines it, is "to create . . . a cognizance in the society of itself, to furnish the means—through clarity of language—for self-appraisal and self-evaluation" (*Interviews* 109). For him a poem is less an aesthetic icon than an instrument of intellection; it seeks not to afford his readers pleasure but to demystify their perception of American reality. Energizing this project are Dorn's emotional alliance with marginalized people, his deep suspicion of mass culture, an obsession with language's fate in postindustrial society, and—most of all—his own extraordinary wit. The literary tools of Dorn's pedagogy have changed frequently and dramatically over the years: lyric verse, realistic fiction, investigative reporting, burlesque epic, and satiric epigrams all act to awaken his audience to "self-appraisal and self-evaluation." In contrast to this variety of genres is the singleness of his attention to the American West. Throughout his career, the geography, history, and mythology of this region have served as the principal site of his vision of the American circumstance.

A native of eastern Illinois, Dorn self-consciously adopted the West as his artistic territory and now considers himself "a poet of the West" (*Interviews* 44). For him the region discloses with stark clarity the original promise and present condition of America. Spiritually at ease in the vast expanse of its landscapes, Dorn ranges widely over the area: the Pacific Northwest, the inter-mountain basin of Montana, Idaho, Nevada, and Utah, the New Mexican Southwest, southern California, the High Plains of Colorado and Wyoming—all prominently figure in his writings. These places mark significant points on an odyssey that Dorn began with high school trips along Route 66 to California and has since continued in a succession of different Western residences. His actual experiences of these locales as well as the other circumstances of his life often become material for his art and contribute directly to his evolution as a writer.

Dorn's literary development may itself be divided into three periods. The initial phase extends from 1957, when his earliest mature work appeared in the *Black Mountain Review*, through 1966, his first full year of residence outside the United States. The writing of this decade insists on the exploitative nature of American capitalism and emphasizes the poor and powerless who are the victims of economic progress. The style is both realistic and declamatory: specific events—typically drawn directly from Dorn's private life—are precisely evoked and become occasions for public statement. Though the abstractions of political discourse are prominent, they spring from particular incidents and remain stylistically subordinate to them. The tone is distinctly personal, sometimes nostalgic, frequently ironic, almost always didactic. The prose of this period includes the naturalistic novel, *The Rites of Passage* (1965), the literary criticism of *What I See in The Maximus Poems* (1960), and the documentary journalism of *The Shoshoneans* (1966). The verse begins with the chastened, elegiac lyricism of such pieces as "The Rick of Green Wood" (1957) and "The Air of June Sings" (*Collected Poems*—henceforth cited, *CP*—3-4,11-12) then develops through the turbulent 1960s toward the highly polemical poems of *Geography* (1965). The work of these years represents what Dorn himself has called his "early sort of adamant practice," in which the writer's voice is aggressively "concerned" and "dogmatic" (*Interviews* 15, 19).

In his second phase Dorn abandoned the strategy of "direct onslaught," having convinced himself that such a "sober sense of the political poem" was "not only very boring but also completely valueless" (*Interviews* 26). This period is bounded at one end by the appearance of *The North Atlantic Turbine* in 1967 and at the other by the 1975 edition of *Slinger*, which revised and collected the separate parts of the poem previously published from 1968 through 1972. In this body of writing Dorn sought different forms of provocation, a search that took him in several related directions. First, he replaced earnest meditations on specific instances of social injustice with cool, theoretical analyses of the general economic forces that determine contemporary history. "The North Atlantic Turbine" (*CP* 179-95), which maps the course of European imperialism from the discovery of America to the war in Vietnam, signals the emergence of this more intellectualized stance. Second, satire, often verging on the burlesque, succeeded sincerity as Dorn's typical manner. "The World Box-Score Cup of 1966" (*CP* 162-78), imaging the conflict between rich and poor nations as an ill-matched sporting event, exemplifies his shift to a comic book brand of humor that relies on witty exaggeration and zany invention.

This turn away from realistic representation is connected to a third stylistic development of these years: Dorn's deepening recognition that language is itself an instrument of political power and his growing efforts to expose its techniques of social control. Most notable in this regard is *Slinger*, which isolates and subverts the dominant culture's use of language to colonize and domesticate consciousness. This comic anti-epic mixes clichés of the Old West with the multiple slangs of mass society to produce a complex parody of contemporary America. It is not only the principal work of Dorn's second period but arguably the major achievement of his career to date.

Though overshadowed by the abstract wit and extravagant invention that distinguish Dorn's work during these years, the personal voice so prominent in his earlier writing is not entirely absent from this period. *Twenty-Four Love Songs* (1969) features intimate pieces that explore the complications of love, while *Songs: Set Two, a Short Count* (1970) projects a drug-induced vision of cosmological unity that transcends socio-economic considerations. In both of these volumes, Dorn has sharply severed the private from the public. No longer is personal experience a bridge to political statement; the domestic has, rather, become a refuge from the world at large.

In the third phase of his career, Dorn retrieves the realism of his earliest work but now fuses it with the cool wit and intellectual sophistication characteristic of his writing since the late 1960s. *Recollections of Gran Apachería* (1974) initiates this new direction. Written while he was completing *Slinger*, this spare, unsentimental account of the Apaches' doomed resistance to the closing of the American frontier shows few traces of *Slinger*'s cartoon fantasy. Instead, historically accurate representations of persons and events are ironically juxtaposed to dramatize the irreconcilable differences between Indian and white cultures.

A similar reliance on carefully observed detail operates in *Hello, La Jolla* (1978) and its companion volume, *Yellow Lola* (1981). Topical in focus and epigrammatic in style, these two books extrapolate Dorn's reactions to southern California into a satiric indictment of contemporary America. Dorn himself regards these writings less as poems than dispatches, on-the-spot reports alerting his audience to the nation's current condition. This journalistic manner also informs the 1983 verse pamphlet, *Captain Jack's Chaps, or Houston/MLA*, an account of the annual meeting of the Modern Language Association of America that is reminiscent of a humor column on a newspaper's op-ed page.

Indeed, the media provides a useful model for Dorn's recent work. By his own testimony, he now spends "a lot of the day monitoring the flow of news" ("Strumming the Language" 86), and he also devotes considerable energy to *Rolling Stock*, the newspaper of literature and politics he has co-edited since 1980. In his efforts to diagnose democracy's health in late capitalist America, immediate events have become for Dorn's art the most telling symptoms of the country's social pathology.

Life

Illinois Years (1929-1950). Dorn was born in the prairie town of Villa Grove on 2 April 1929, the first year of the Great Depression. He never knew his father, who abandoned the family. His mother and stepfather, a mechanic, were poor, frequently moving among factory and farm jobs in eastern Illinois and southern

Michigan, typically living in rented houses and working lands owned by others. For most of the first eight grades, Dorn attended a one-room schoolhouse and spent much time with his grandmother, whose husband is the railroad man memorialized by "Obituary" (*CP* 47-49). In high school, Dorn edited the student paper, worked on the local town newspaper, and wrote a few short stories. At sixteen, he made the first of many trips to California, an event recalled in "Palms, Victory, Triumph, Excellence" (*Hello, La Jolla* 91).

He attended the University of Illinois at Champaign-Urbana for two years (1949-1950), where he was in the general studies program, though his major interest at the time was architecture. Through his roommate's connections, Dorn first visited the Pacific Northwest, spending the summer of 1949 working at a Boeing plant in Seattle. During the next summer he took classes at Eastern Illinois and learned from Ray Obermayr, his art professor there, about the experimental Black Mountain College in North Carolina. Dissatisfied with the state university and anxious to maintain his student deferment from military service in Korea, he left Illinois in the fall of 1950 to enroll at Black Mountain.

These early years in Illinois were informed by rural poverty and its emotional desolation. Their imprint was deep, producing attitudes that animate much of Dorn's writing. His conviction of the injustice of the American economic system, anger at the suffering it inflicts, and distrust of the privileged classes that benefit from it may be traced to this period. "On the Debt My Mother Owed to Sears Roebuck" (*CP* 46-47) powerfully evokes the sorrow of dispossessed farm life, while "The Sense Comes Over Me, and the Waning Light of Man by the 1st National Bank" (*CP* 153-56) directly links his own family's deprivation to the country's financial structure.

Dorn's emotional distance from society also originates in the harshness of his Illinois youth. This acute personal deracination makes the nomadic life of the open road Dorn's most natural state. And it underlies as well both his affinity for other lonely drifters and his belief that "the non-property-owning, alienated, excluded, nowhere-to-go stranger" is "the *only* figure that represents the rectitude of the human condition" (*Views* 13-14).

Another important facet of Dorn's temperament that reflects his rural boyhood is sensitivity to the interplay between landscape and human behavior. "The Sparrow Sky" and "Goodbye to Illinois" (*CP* 14-15, 17) dramatize the powerful physical presence of the plains. Both are Midwestern versions of an interest in cultural geography that Dorn later transposes to the West.

Black Mountain Years (1950-1955). When Dorn arrived at Black Mountain in 1950, the small, arts-oriented school was in a state of uneasy transition. While still radically committed to communal and intellectual openness, the previous year it had suffered the resignation of Josef Albers, the avant-garde painter and apologist for modernism whose leadership had been critical to the institution almost from the day of its founding in 1933. Albers' influence persisted into Dorn's initial year, which was devoted largely to courses in the visual arts. But more important than particular classroom activities was the impact of Dorn's first encounter with an urban, Eastern sensibility: this "city expression and sophistication" with its "very advanced ideas of how one lives" sharply challenged his "very country" Midwestern past (*Interviews* 12).

In the summer of 1951, before completing his studies at Black Mountain, Dorn decided to leave. He began a prolonged trip into the West, wandering around Kansas, Wyoming, and the Northwest, where he met and married his first wife, Helene. Most of their time was spent in Washington: here he worked in the forests and was especially impressed by the politically active loggers—Wobblies and other Marxist workers—whom he met.

In the fall of 1954 Dorn returned to Black Mountain, fully determined to finish his degree. And circumstances were clearly different: he himself had become a family man with responsibility for children, and leadership of the college was now firmly lodged in the charismatic personality of Charles Olson. This unorthodox Melville scholar and proponent of a projective, open field poetics assumed the rectorship in 1953 and immediately began shifting the curriculum away from the fine arts toward writing. Also a brilliant teacher, Olson possessed an uncanny ability to discover a student's talents and tailor a program specifically around them. This he did for Dorn, whose participation in Olson's composition class evolved into a master-pupil relation that both provoked Dorn to serious writing and also became, as he says, "totally responsible for the activity of my mind so far as I can use it" (*Interviews* 14). In the summer of 1955, he passed his qualifying examinations, with Robert Creeley, whom Olson had just appointed editor of the college's new *Black Mountain Review,* acting as Dorn's outside examiner. That September he graduated.

The Black Mountain years broadened Dorn's knowledge of places and ideas, gave intellectual depth to his attitudes, and focused his literary attentions. Under Olson's tutelage he formalized interest in the West, launching his lifelong search after "what will identify the West in some big conceptual sense" (*Interviews* 30). The methodology for this pursuit he acquired from *A Bibliography on America for Ed Dorn,* which Olson wrote in response to his request for guidance in studying the West. The multidisciplinary approach Olson urged combines rigorous research with deep personal involvement, demanding intense scholarly as well as imaginative energy.

Typical of this stance was Olson's recommending Carl Sauer's "Morphology of Landscape" (in his collected essays, *Land and Life*).

Based on close examination of man's local interaction with the physical environment, Sauer's model of cultural geography taught Dorn to subordinate poetic descriptions of scenery to historical and economic analysis of the human habitation of particular landscapes. This practice of deferring aesthetics to facts and engaging subjects with passionate literalness was Dorn's true education at Black Mountain.

The college also constituted Dorn's first literary community, providing that network of personal contacts which encouraged and published his early work. When in 1960 this circle of writers emerged onto the national scene as the Black Mountain poets in Donald Allen's celebrated *New American Poetry* anthology, Dorn appeared beside Olson, Creeley, and others associated with both the school and its famous *Black Mountain Review*. What united this loosely knit group was not a shared stylistic or thematic program but rather friendship, antagonism to academic verse, and a common belief in literature's absolute seriousness. Three decades after Olson closed the college in 1957, the Black Mountain label is still used to identify Dorn. But though many of the individual ties from those years remain, the social cohesion created by Olson's magnetic personality was a momentary phenomenon, and Dorn long ago began pursuing his distinctly separate artistic concerns.

Sojourning in the West (1955-1965). For two years after his graduation from Black Mountain, Dorn moved nomadically about the trans-mountain West, pausing in his travels for a longer stay in San Francisco. During this period he started to write continuously and to regard himself as a poet. In 1957 he settled with Helene and the children in Burlington, Washington. *The Rites of Passage* is an autobiographical depiction of their life in this Skagit Valley town. The novel intersperses the family's struggles against grinding poverty with Dorn's memories of an earlier Depression-ridden

Illinois. This splicing of different times and places powerfully projects the impression of permanent suffering at the margins of the American social system. Or, as Dorn states his point in another work of this period: "not a damn / thing / ever changes: the cogs that turn this machine are set / a thousand miles on plumb" (*CP* 77).

In 1959 Dorn moved to Santa Fe, where he worked as an assistant to the reference librarian at the New Mexico State Library. With an extensive book collection at hand, he confirmed the habit of historical research on the West that would continue to inform his writing. "Death While Journeying" and "Ledyard: The Exhaustion of Sheer Distance" (*CP* 49-54) spring directly from his reading at this time. The first imagines Meriwether Lewis' last fatal trip, the other recounts the explorer John Ledyard's career, and both celebrate migratory temperaments that prefer the rootless freedom of open space to fixed settlement.

"The Land Below" (*CP* 57-73) furnishes a more immediate index of Dorn's Santa Fe sojourn. "In america," this loosely structured poem argues, "every art has to reach toward some / clarity," and Dorn consequently proposes an aggressive "transfer of knowledge" about the nation's morality. Moving quickly through a variety of incidents specific to these New Mexico days, Dorn exposes the cruelty and shallowness of the local white culture. To counter its brute acquisitiveness, mindless faith in technology, and addiction to political cant, Dorn offers the figures of Henry David Thoreau and an anonymous Indian elder accidentally met on a fourth of July picnic in Taos. Both embody that "mystique of the real" which respects "our lovely Earth" as the actual ground of the self and knows the New World to be "our reservoir of Life." But ironically, what Dorn finds most remarkable about the beauty embodied in Thoreau and the ancient Indian is "that you / can never return to it. It never / exists again, once having been there." And it is in this state of unresolved tension, caught between an irredeemable present and an unrecoverable past, that Dorn stops the poem. The sentimental solution suppressed, the recalcitrant facts uncompromisingly asserted—this tough-minded refusal to romanticize is an early and abiding hallmark of Dorn's sensibility.

In the fall of 1961 Dorn again moved, having accepted a teaching position at Idaho State University. Creeley, then living in Albuquerque, helped to relocate Dorn and his family in Pocatello, where they remained until the summer of 1965. Loneliness and disaffection are recurrent emotional notes of these years, and they sound poignantly in such poems as "Christ of the Sparrows Help Me!," "This afternoon was unholy," and "Dark Ceiling" (*CP* 135-37, 141-42). But the period was also marked by greater public visibility for Dorn's poetry. LeRoi Jones, the black writer and political activist now known as Amiri Baraka, was Dorn's principal correspondent at this time, and he published through his Totem Press in New York the first books of verse, *The Newly Fallen* (1961) and *Hands Up!* (1964). The latter collection and *Geography* (1965) frequently incorporate elements of Dorn's Idaho experience.

Deeply imbedded in these years is "Idaho Out" (*CP* 107-22), a long meditation organized about a roundtrip between Pocatello and Missoula, Montana. The alienation that governed "The Land Below" persists, but Dorn's understanding of the reasons for his disillusion clearly advances. He adopts Sauer's method for analyzing the environment's impact on culture and discovers that the open expanses of the Western landscape encourage the society's worst desires for quick profits. Tragically, the West's seductive geography both invites the economic exploitation that destroys its land and stimulates the greed that pollutes its psyche. The region thus suffers a double damnation: matching the material defacement of "the arco desert and / what's there / of the leakage of newclear seance" is the spiritual emptiness of a citizenry disfigured by "the dirtiest / of human proportions." Dorn does acknowledge some contrary forces: occasionally, a woman like his "Beauty of North Fork," and a place like the "lovely" Fort Benton, Montana, are superior to the region's usual "life of petty retreat." Yet ultimately, Idaho emerges in Dorn's mind as "truly the West / as no other place / ruined by an ambition and religion / cut, by a cowboy use of her nearly virgin self." The poem concludes by noting that Idaho is also the birthplace of Ezra Pound and the last home of Ernest Hemingway—writers whose conscription of literature into the service of cultural reform Dorn himself shares. They act here, however, not as models but warnings against the danger of artistic presumption. For both had heroically assumed for their work the task of spiritual redemption, and Dorn is quick to recall that the signature of Pound's career was Fascism and that Hemingway's ended in suicide. His more modest ambition, as "Idaho Out" announces, is to be a "classical poet" who examines the ethics of man's social behavior, and he consequently rejects romantic claims for art's mythic or religious function.

When in 1965 Dorn departed for England, he could look back on a decade during which he had successfully applied the principles learned at Black Mountain to an increasingly sophisticated engagement of the West. Two aspects of this development warrant emphasis. First, Dorn conceives the West to be an irreversibly fallen world, controlled by the politics of private property and victimized by the technology of mineral extraction. In this respect, it is an extension of the Midwest, and in a late poem, "The Stripping of the River," the two regions together define the "center of our true richness" that has been drained of its "metal and grain and fuel" by the financial interests of the coasts (*CP* 267). Though they are linked by their common exploitation, the West also differs from the Midwest, since its lack of urban industrialization leaves the physical abuse more spectacularly visible.

Dorn's personal attitude toward the West during these years also deserves emphasis. He regards it not as a home but an artistic laboratory and remains a stranger in the towns he inhabits. Sitting on his porch in Santa Fe and contemplating his relation to the surrounding scene, Dorn explains, "the removals / are what I am trying to pronounce, that they / are my case" (*CP* 76). And an essay written in Pocatello argues even more generally the West's resistance to human community: "The native westerner," Dorn insists, "is the most sad man in the world. He has no where to go. The West is not a home" (*Views* 59).

British Interlude (1965-1970). The English poet and literary critic Donald Davie was the catalyst for Dorn's move to the University of Essex in the fall of 1965. Davie, then a vice chancellor at this newly chartered institution, had met Dorn in Pocatello during a tour of the United States the preceding academic year, and recruited him for the school's fledgling literature department. For four of the next five years Dorn was Visiting Professor of American Literature at Essex, the first two as a Fulbright Lecturer. He interrupted his service during 1968-69, first by a fall spent in European travel and then by a residency as Visiting Poet at the University of Kansas in Lawrence over the spring semester of 1969. Though Dorn's years in Britain were relatively few, the stay nonetheless had important consequences for both his work and personal life.

The North Atlantic Turbine (1967) tellingly mirrors this period. The volume bears a triple dedication that signals the new set of literary connections Dorn established in England. Besides Davie, he pays tribute to J.H. Prynne and Tom Raworth, writers who disrupt literature's historical ties with formal beauty to concentrate instead on its ability to open non-aesthetic, broadly political avenues into experience. Also sharing Raworth and Prynne's interest in poetry's ideological dimensions was Gordon Brotherson, the English translator Dorn met at Essex and with whom he soon began collaborating. Their first joint effort, *Our Word: Guerrilla Poems from Latin America* (1968), was produced with assistance from José Emilio Pacheco, a Mexican writer in residence at Essex during 1967-68 whose poem, *Tree Between Two Walls*, Dorn and Brotherson also translated together (1969). In addition to these foreign colleagues, the American Tom Clark, at that time a student at Essex and now a prominent figure on the California poetry scene, came to share Dorn's fascination with the West. Indeed, Dorn introduces Clark's recent collection of verse, *A Short Guide to the High Plains* (1980), with a scathing essay on the region's casual violence.

Dorn's reaction to England and its impact on his thought are everywhere apparent in *The North Atlantic Turbine* but are especially striking in "Oxford" (*CP* 195-216), a poem that proceeds by dismantling the central premise of topographical verse. Retaining many elements characteristic of the loco-descriptive genre, "Oxford" opens with a train ride into the city, continues through an account of the area's physical geography, an inventory of its tourist attractions, and a transcription of a conversation with some of its citizens, finally concluding with a meditation on this university center's sociohistorical significance. But instead of following literary convention and celebrating Oxford's uniqueness, the poem demonstrates that the traditional concept of place is both sentimental and corrupt, vacated of meaning by the international triumph of American capitalism. So successful has the United States' commercial empire become since World War II, that language is now universally homogenized and essential local differences effaced. Today "*America / is* the world"—its commodity culture "Everybody's idea." The world naively imagined it could "have the *Idea*" of America "without the thing," forgetting the "oldest danger, that to *think* / is to be locked inside the thing." Oxford, no less than Europe at large, is, in effect, a suburb of American consciousness. "We are *all*," Dorn hence remarks with reference to the war then raging in Vietnam, "in the *da nang*," and this condition deflects the final focus of "Oxford" away from the English city to "the new / world," which he gloomily concludes "was an evil world— / it should never have been discovered."

This recognition of the global reach of American economic values was a major consequence of Dorn's encounter with British culture. Not only did it internationalize his understanding of the American West and encourage a more theoretical perspective on politics, it also depersonalized Dorn's anger. Symptomatic of both tendencies is the chilling wit of the first section of "Oxford." Titled simply "Fornication," it employs baldly sexual diction to present the beauty of upper class women as a commodity manufactured for exchange in the world's marketplace of colonial power. The "imperialism / implied by their shapely legs," the poem observes with grim irony, exists "by no other act than Murder."

This cool, abstract eye born of Dorn's discovery of the American hegemony does not, however, control *Twenty-Four Love Songs* (1969), which commemorates his relation with his new wife, Jennifer Dunbar. Written just before the couple's first trip together to the United States late in 1968, this sequence of personal lyrics is charged with an emotional intensity that projects a quite different image of the years in England. While the usual difficulties of Dorn's intellectualized, virtually metaphysical style persist, the book's surges of erotic energy distinguish it.

Several years later there was a coda to this British interlude, when the family returned to England for the academic year 1974-75, and Dorn again taught American literature at Essex. *Manchester Square* (1975), a book produced in collaboration with his wife, springs from a visit to the West End of London during that year. In this collection of verse, the personal and political again intersect, as they had in Dorn's earliest work. Within the volume's brief expanse, the tensions of the previous stay in England relax: the private aspects of *Manchester Square* are more casually domestic than those of *Twenty-Four Love Songs*, while its public dimension, though still critical, is less strident than *The North Atlantic Turbine*.

Years of Academic Touring and a Return to the Rockies (1970-). One of the last poems in *The North Atlantic Turbine* is "An Idle Visitation." The title refers not to the poem's subject but its manner of composition: "That particular poem just came," Dorn explained, "I wrote it and I didn't even know what I was doing" (*Interviews* 25). Conspicuously different from the book's other pieces, this cartoon-like narrative fragment announced, in fact, the beginning of *Slinger*, the massive project that would absorb Dorn's creative energy from 1967 until 1974. Though conceived and begun in England, the poem was largely written after Dorn's return to the United States, which began with an appointment at Northeastern Illinois University in Chicago from the fall of 1970 through the winter of 1971.

After travelling about Mexico in the spring of 1972, Dorn settled in San Francisco, participating in the city's famous North Beach poetry scene. More critically for his career, he also formed close ties with the West Coast's small press publishers, most notably Holbrook Teter and Michael Myers, printers at Wingbow Press which issued the complete *Slinger*, and Donald Allen of Four Seasons Foundation, which produced the important collected editions of Dorn's poetry and prose. These San Francisco years were, however, regularly interrupted by academic jobs of varying tenures. In 1973-74 Dorn was on the faculty of Kent State University in Ohio, while the fall quarter of 1974 found him as Regent's Lecturer at the University of California-Riverside and the winter quarter of 1976 as Writer in Residence at the University of California-San Diego. Throughout this period he also read frequently on campuses, taking advantage of *Slinger*'s popularity among students to supplement his income. Then, in 1977 Dorn's peripatetic relation to the academy took a different turn when he accepted a post at the University of Colorado. What began as another temporary appointment evolved into a permanent arrangement, and for more than a decade Dorn has lived in the Rocky Mountain city of Boulder, serving as a member of Colorado's English Department and teaching in its Creative Writing Program.

While numerous poems directly reflect the circumstances of Dorn's life since his return from England, there is, perhaps, no better published index of the last ten years of this period than *Rolling Stock*, the occasional newspaper he edits with his wife. Its title is drawn from the technical vocabulary of the railroad industry, which figures throughout Dorn's work as a symbol of the economic forces that corrupted the West. The newspaper's heterogeneous contents combine literary and political matters, acting as an encyclopedia of Dorn's ongoing concerns. Regular columns on medicine, the law, cinema, books, and golf—a sport Dorn himself now seriously pursues—are mixed with a steady stream of cultural satire, including frequent cartoons, social commentary on issues ranging from the legal rights of American Indians to prostitution and pornography, and reports—often first-hand—from troubled Third World countries. Though the variety may suggest any general interest magazine, *Rolling Stock* is emphatically oppositional and outrageously irreverent of conventional wisdom, recalling the tone and style of the 1960s underground press.

In addition to its role as an intellectual inventory, *Rolling Stock* also functions as a directory of Dorn's personal literary circle. Among regular contributors are writer and artist Fielding Dawson, a classmate from Black Mountain, the experimental film maker, Stan Brakhage, an old friend from New Mexico, and Tom Raworth, J.H. Prynne, and Tom Clark, continuing connections from the years in England. There are also frequent items by newer ties such as Richard "Dobro Dick" Dillo, the hero of *Captain Jack's Chaps*, and the postmodernist novelist Steve Katz, a colleague in Colorado's creative writing program. Occasional appearances are made by other longstanding acquaintances, including Creeley, Ray Obermayr, Dorn's adviser from undergraduate days in Illinois, and Amiri Baraka, the publisher of his first books. For each issue Dorn himself writes a column, "Salients": these brief notices of new publications reflect other alliances he has on the literary scene.

Reinforcing *Rolling Stock's* value as an indicator of the current directions of Dorn's thought are the editorials he sometimes offers. More rarely, the newspaper prints his latest poetry or an article, like his account of the 3rd Annual Cowboy Poetry Gathering featured in the newspaper's thirteenth number (1987). From his early days in Pocatello editing the magazine *Wild Dog*, Dorn has taken periodical publication seriously, and his attention to *Rolling Stock* testifies to the consistency of his commitment to this mode of communication.

Early Adamant Period: 1956-1966

Dorn's first separately published work, *What I See in The Maximus Poems* (1960), is also one of his most important statements of artistic principles. In *The Maximus Poems* Olson had sought at epic length to repossess both historically and imaginatively his native Gloucester, Massachusetts. While Dorn's pamphlet testifies eloquently to Olson's success, it also declares his own identity as a writer.

The crux of the essay is its unequivocal separation of man from nature: "one of the loveliest qualities of Western Man," Dorn insists, is "that he is abstract . . . . as far purely away from nature as he can get" (*Views* 37). This deliberately anti-romantic stance contradicts the fashionable 1950s cult of Oriental philosophy, which abandoned reason and absorbed the conscious mind into the physical universe. Dorn's contrary premise is that the material environment is, in fact deadening to man, and he promotes instead the vitality of will and ego. Only by exercising these uniquely human faculties, Dorn argues, was Olson able to transform the objective presence of Gloucester into "a social world of intention" that is a fully habitable home for man. Since for Dorn human creativity alone is meaningful, he alters Joyce Kilmer's familiar line and argues that " 'only man can make a tree' " (*Views* 36, 38).

But while *What I See in The Maximus Poems* promotes the ego as the custodian of community and history, the essay also recognizes it to be "a dangerous thing" and acknowledges as well that man's removal from nature is the source of "his intense ugliness" (*Views* 40, 37). Such paradoxes are at the center of Dorn's temperament. He is the champion of abstract intelligence who is hypersensitive to the social abuse of intellect and the celebrant of "what is decent and lovely and dignified in man," who nonetheless knows how rarely this promise is achieved.

Indeed, the essay qualifies Olson's success with the contrary example of Haniel Long, the New Mexico writer whose work was minor precisely because the cultural geography of the Southwest prevented any human "concordance of place" (*Views* 34). Dorn offers Long as "the specimen of a radical mind with no home, no anchorage" and suggests that the loss he suffered is inevitably risked by every writer whose territory is the West—himself included. From *What I See in The Maximus Poems* Dorn thus emerges as an artist committed to a human universe that harmonizes nature with man, but who is also edgily aware of the excesses of both that imperil so delicate a construct. Dorn's is a difficult position, tense with paradox, unrelentingly skeptical, and absolutely intolerant of solutions that are emotionally easy or intellectually lazy.

This complex play of critical thought is already present in Dorn's first collection of verse. The poems of *The Newly Fallen* (1961) move among several distinct but complementary tones and themes. Personal melancholy—associated with regret for vanished innocence or missed opportunity—informs many pieces. "And Thus" and "Our Camp" (*CP* 36, 29) cast this sadness into parables of a mythic fall from original bliss, while "If it should ever come" registers the pathos of friends' lives by measuring their emptiness against the prospective end of time (*CP* 38). The most touching of these poems is "Sousa," which recalls a May Day celebration in rural Illinois when the composer's music perfectly captured Dorn's feeling "hopeful, and kind / merrily and possible." This fond memory of Sousa's "triumph of a march / in which no one / is injured" is, however, irrevocably isolated from the present by Dorn's disillusioned image of the contemporary Southwest, where the "desire to disintegrate the Earth" dominates and there is "no purity, no endeavor / toward human grace" (*CP* 22-26).

The sentimentality Dorn flirts with and suppresses in "Sousa" does not enter a second group of poems in *The Newly Fallen* that are motivated less by nostalgia for a lost America than by anger at current socio-economic conditions. "The Argument Is" satirizes the pious pretensions of rich people's charity by emphasizing the psychological distress deprived children suffer by wearing cast-off "clothes fitting as casually as though / they were / stolen / from the wealth / of the nation" (*CP* 30-31). "Prayers for the People of the World" attacks another form of hypocrisy, the use of religious rhetoric to mask society's cynical exploitation of the poor, who are treated like "the vitamin not stored" that "goes out in the urine of all endeavor" (*CP* 35). The most vigorous of these polemical efforts is "The Biggest Killing." A meditation on the Trinity site in New Mexico, where the first atomic bomb was exploded, the poem attacks both the nation's "lethal metric bubbles of science" and the American government that is so "decayed, so cynical / it cannot smell the blood it lifts / and drinks" (*Newly Fallen* 15-18).

Countering the pessimism of these poems of loss and indictment is a third set in Dorn's first book that quietly celebrates the beauty of life at the margins of society. These include "The Common Lot" (*Newly Fallen* 27), which along with "The Biggest Killing" does not appear in the *Collected Poems*, and "Like a Message on Sunday," a truly tender prayer for the oppressed (*CP* 28-29). Also in this group is the volume's opening poem, "Geranium," which links Dorn's fleeting sight of an Indian woman at a bus stop near Burlington, Washington, with the lowly geranium flower to declare his "love of common object" (*CP* 13).

Dorn's next collection, *Hands Up!* (1964), announces by the words of its title the explicitly Western focus of much of its verse. The phrase invokes the language of heroic bravura which Hollywood invented to represent the West, and the particular poem which bears the injunction "Hands Up," mercilessly explores the discrepancy between this celluloid image of moralized violence and the reality of the New West, "where friends / cremate each other / to make room / and phosphate / is one lucky factory owner's / element" (*CP* 84-85). The assault on the contemporary West continues in "Wagon Wheels," a sardonic account of suburban cowboys who own "ranch style houses" and keep horses like pets (*CP* 40); and in "Trail Creek, Aug. 11, the Reason of Higher Powers," which parodies the sanctimonious logic of the West's emerging commercial classes, who presume divine blessings for their middle class interests (*CP* 42-43). Rewriting another cliché of frontier rhetoric, "Home on the Range, February, 1962" extends the historical scope of Dorn's argument. Interpreting nineteenth-century "homesteads" as "america's first subdivisions," the poem characterizes the entire settlement of the West as nothing less than "a hundred years of planned greed" (*CP* 43-44).

The political premise motivating Dorn's judgments in these poems is stated in "A Too Hopefully Bold Measure," which explores the shift from the gritty entrepreneurs of California's gold rush days to the current world of corporate capitalism, where "men clothed in soft wool" promote "the manifest destiny of Rand" (*CP* 77-78). Though the poem reflects the tendency of popular historians to celebrate the bold individualism of the era of robber barons, Dorn refuses to romanticize the past. He suggests instead that the institution of property—by legalizing and encouraging the acquisitive instinct—is itself destructive of both man and nature. His inelegant but forceful conclusion is that "all are screwed and tatooed / with all economies."

The losses which the profit motive have levied on the West are not only explored in "The Land Below," the longest piece in *Hands Up!*, but are also the subject of other poems in the volume. "In the Morning" summons an image of Southwestern rural poverty, with its "silent rising holocaust of down people," all casualties of "the mock buzzing of a sound economy" (*CP* 56). "Los Mineros" examines the remains of a New Mexican ghost town to dramatize the human and geographical wastage of the mining industry. Even more emotionally charged, "The Air of June Sings" revitalizes the hackneyed conventions of the graveyard elegy to disclose the inhumanity of the West's archetypal pioneer, who used his commercial success to elevate himself above common sentiment. His pretentious monument stands apart from "the small quiet stones of the unpreposterous dead" and bespeaks the power of business to fracture democracy and erect alienating class barriers (*CP* 11-12).

Hands Up! also contains a number of more strictly personal pieces, among which "Oh Don't Ask Why" is especially notable. Dedicated to his wife Helene and recapitulating the years of their family's Western sojourn, the poem expresses Dorn's sense of rootlessness amid "these rickety geographies / we knew better than to call home." It records as well the private cost of his political concerns, acknowledging how he "did waste / our lives, giving way / foolishly to public thoughts, / large populations" (*CP* 82-84). Another important personal poem from this period, *From Gloucester Out* (1964), pays tribute to Olson and that strictness of artistic attention which enabled him to absorb the world fully into himself. It also poignantly states Dorn's own abiding alienation, even in the company of dearest friends: "Pure existence," he regretfully admits, "will never be possible for me / even with the men I love / This is / the guilt / that kills me / My adulterated presence" (*CP* 86-91).

From Gloucester Out appeared first as a separately printed pamphlet a year before Dorn's next volume of poems, *Geography* (1965), but it was not included there, even though the new collection was dedicated to Olson. The distinctly personal, almost domestic tone of that act of homage does, however, continue in a large group of poems situated at the very center of *Geography*. Dorn typically uses the term "song" to designate these intimate lyrics that are like narrative fragments of his life in Pocatello. Though essentially expressions of emotional pain, they are by no means easy to understand. This difficulty is, perhaps, as significant as the verse's content, for it reveals a special dimension of Dorn's distrust of the dominant culture—a skeptical remove from canonical literature's diction and conventions. Many of the songs are dense with literary language and employ very traditional techniques. "Song: Heat," for example, uses allegory to connect love and politics, while "Song" ("This afternoon was unholy") opens with an accomplished imitation of William Butler Yeats' romanticism. But both also assert their ironic distance from these historically sanctioned styles, subverting their own modes of expression and vastly complicating the reader's response.

This denial of cultural authority is especially interesting in "Six Views from the Same Window of the Northside Grocery" (*CP* 123-25), another poem addressed to his wife Helene on the topic of their "life gone terribly goddam lonely." Its title recalls Wallace Stevens' famous "Thirteen Ways of Looking at a Blackbird," and the poem appears, indeed, to follow the prescriptions of Stevens' art. The window through which Dorn stares parallels the language he uses to record his impressions—each is a medium that can be adjusted to change the appearance of the subject being framed. The poem at first treats the window as transparent and language as literal, then proceeds to extend the limits of both, elaborating metaphors to alter representation and move toward the symbolical transfiguration of the world which Stevens proposes. But having established the grounds for such a verbal redemption of their unhappy isolation, Dorn reverses himself, denying imagination's power to change anything: "Thus a window / is that seemingly clear opening our tested knowledges / pass through and the world shakes not at all / before the weight of our disappointments." This candid acknowledgment of art's practical ineffectiveness stems from Dorn's anti-romanticism. Language is properly, he insists, an instrument of analysis and literature a tool of intellection: their symbolic reach becomes instantly futile or dangerous when it divorces itself from accurate perception and fabricates an ideal realm apart from empirical experience.

Language's parallel and equally insidious ability to vacate reality of meaning occasions the group of poems that opens *Geography*. Acts of social diagnosis, they spring from Dorn's disillusioned rage at American public life during the turmoil of the late 1960s. While the longest of the pieces, "Idaho Out," is located in the West, others are focused nationally. "A Letter, in the Meantime, Not to be Mailed Tonight" and "Inauguration Poem #2" (*CP* 99-105) explicitly attack President Lyndon Johnson's administration, though their central concern is neither domestic nor foreign policy but the violent emptiness of American culture. Both portray the country as a spiritual wilderness inhabited by ghostly outcasts. "Spooks," Dorn calls these citizens of a nightmare America, whose world is haunted by racism, class conflict, genocide, and the profit calculus of Wall Street, all of which are, however, so thoroughly absorbed into the verbal and visual rhetoric of the mass media that they no longer seem real. "A Letter, in the Meantime, Not to be Mailed Tonight" raises the possibility that art itself has lost its substantiality and been co-opted "to keep us apart but more than that, to keep / our senses apart, to make dormant at least / and at best to make wrecked" man's capacity to "track / with the capturing powers of our own love / the expanding universe."

Geography's vivisection of the American body politic is performed most completely in "The Problem of the Poem for My Daughter, Left Unsolved" (*CP* 92-99). Dorn's ungainly title as well as the awkward style of his text self-consciously play off of Yeats' magisterial "A Prayer for My Daughter." Yeats sought to exorcise from his child's future the destructive hatred of Irish politics, which the poem embodies in the image of Maude Gonne. A similar role is played in Dorn's meditation by an anonymous woman he accidentally meets in an Idaho grocery store and by the aviatrix Amelia

Earhart. Like Maude Gonne, these female "figures of despair" are victims, though not of the excesses of nationalist fervor but rather of "the total pestilence" of the American spirit. In the United States, Dorn argues, "there is no intelligence," only a mindless worship of fashion and technology, marked in his poem by the failed femininity of the one woman's "sagging nylons" and by the other's transvestite career as "a weirdly technical Icarus." For Dorn, ours is finally a "provided nation," in which the cult of material comfort renders pain superficial and reduces desire to mechanical technique. In this "totally onanized culture," social definition recedes into media manipulation and everyone remains "oblivious" to the "brutal economic calculus" that sustains a country "where those who care / are the damned of the earth."

Yeats' challenge had been to protect a heritage of aristocratic courtesy from the incursions of contemporary history. Integral to that tradition was the premise that literature is an autonomous artifact removed from the world of vulgar event. For Yeats to compose a poem that displays an aesthetic wholeness superior to the disorder of its immediate environment is, in effect, a political statement, his means of asserting the past's control of the present and maintaining his daughter's inheritance. But the benediction he could pronounce through the transformative power of romantic symbol is not available to Dorn, who has nothing to preserve but "a memory / saturated by defeat." In his "technologically provisioned" land of "mail food ads" and "manufactured Galateability," he must, in fact, vigorously resist the temptation of beauty and devote himself instead to exposing this "nest of the most corrupted notion thus far: America!" Because words are unable to create a legacy worth conferring, Dorn concludes, "I can tell my daughter no secret."

But language may be used polemically to rally animosity against foes and support for allies. And this oratorical function shapes many of the poems that conclude *Geography*. These are, in effect, rhetorical acts of revolution that anticipate the verbal warfare Dorn and Gordon Brotherson honor by their translations in *Our Word: Guerrilla Poems from Latin America* (1968). "The Smug Never Silent Guns of the Enemy" (*CP* 145-46) sets the tone for this final section of the volume. Suggesting that intercontinental missiles, commodity price fixing, mass produced insecticides, and news broadcasts are different weapons in the arsenal of economic and political oppression, the poem mocks the insane logic of this military-industrial thinking through the character of a "squat madeyed colonel" who "announces the way to peace thru war and shoots the moderator." "Eugene Delacroix Says" (*CP* 148-50) opens with the proposition that poverty-ridden Appalachia is a contemporary American version of Europe's ancient class divisions, then declares the inevitability of that day when the wealthy's "ugly eyes prolix with beefsteak will be / snatched out," and finally ends with a malicious prayer against the revolution's prospective victims. "Song: Venceremos" (*CP* 150-153), whose Spanish cry that "we shall overcome" states the poem's subversive intent, follows a similar movement from social commentary to injunction. After examining the United States' imperialist intervention in South America, it offers prescriptions for cultural action designed to recover "a specific measure of respect" for exploited workers.

"For the New Union Dead in Alabama" (*CP* 160-161), a pained meditation on the human costs of the civil rights movement, closes *Geography* with a formal curse. Invoking the Biblical Rose of Sharon as an emblem of the redemptive power of sacrificial love, the poem echoes with deliberate irony the ecstatic rhythms and imagery of the *Song of Songs*. But Dorn's is no lush vision of spiritual consummation. Rather "in the desert / of american life," our nation's "gelding mentality" tolerates only a "gelding culture," which violently strips the flower of its petals, leaving only "the thorn / in the throat of our national hypocrisy." This world of "raw greed" renders martyrdom meaningless and leaves Dorn with only a cry of damnation: "o rose / of priceless beauty / refrain from our shores / suffocate the thin isthmus / of our mean land, / cast us back / into isolation."

Dorn's despair about American society is less strident in *The Rites of Passage* (1965), which appeared the same year as *Geography*. Though the tone is muted by the low-keyed style of this fictionalized autobiography, the judgment remains identical. Structured around Carl and Mary Wyman's arrival in a small rural town north of Seattle and their departure a year and a half later, the novel proceeds not by conventional plot but through a series of episodes that reveal the history and tenor of the Wymans' lives and those of their friends. Carl is Dorn's image of himself. A college graduate whose working class background has left him leary of the psychological price exacted by bourgeois prosperity, he brought his family to the Skagit Valley community seeking pastoral relief from their urban past. James McCarty, a self-destructive refugee of the middle class, is an alcoholic carpenter married to Ramona, a tubercular but vibrant Eskimo woman who continues to fight the welfare agencies that deprived her of her native heritage. And Billy Hendersson is the tough, nomadic survivor whose anger at injustice and compassion for its victims make him the book's hero.

Thematically, *The Rites of Passage*, or more appropriately, *By the Sound*—which is Dorn's original and preferred title—examines the contemporary fate of the American dream of self-reliance. This powerful national desire to live in the heart of nature free from the entrapments of social and financial obligation animates all of Dorn's principal characters. Each in his or her own way avoids that "limbo" inhabited by people of every station from "the nightwatchman to the executive" who barter "time and looks and attention" for the respectability of holding jobs "as a matter of habit" (*By the Sound* 64). Hendersson is the classic exemplar of their common revolt against conformity. Like Huck Finn—and, indeed, Twain's romance is one of the few books Billy owns—he severs his domestic ties, lured by the frontier's promised freedom. But he soon discovers that the "new world" he expects in Alaska is "the same old story": "It's closed off," he explains, "it's a land of business men," and "his boyhood dream" ends in a Sitka prison, Billy ironically guilty of no more than associating with the poor (161, 163).

With its stump farms and abandoned buildings, nature in the Skagit Valley has also been conspicuously converted to real estate. In Dorn's image of post-World War II America, there are, in fact, no unowned Walden Ponds to which would-be Thoreaus may freely retreat. The price of refusing to participate in the nation's system of private property has become a debilitating poverty that sadly diminishes life. Nowhere in the novel is the "damn meanness" (51) suffered by Dorn's self-reliant outsiders more obvious than in the chapter "The Deer," which converts the stock male romance of the hunt into a grotesque farce of economic desperation. Bumbling feverishly about the woods in search of fresh meat, Billy and Carl finally succeed in bagging their quarry, which proves, however, not to be the buck they thought they were stalking but a helpless cow strayed from its pen. But while masculine pride has been devastated, honesty is still present. Hendersson candidly admits the nature of his act: "I'm just like those union officials—a petty thief" (164).

Throughout *By the Sound*, such dispassionate frankness governs Dorn's voice, which steadfastly refrains from sentimentalizing poverty, or even encouraging sorrow at its depredations. For the book is less concerned to engage readers emotionally than to ground its own ethical judgments in an open, unprejudiced confrontation with fact. Typical of Dorn's strategy is his portrait of Ramona McCarty, which unsparingly catalogs her drunkenness, sloppiness, and self-defeating temper—thus risking complicity with the most vicious forms of racial stereotyping. But honesty here lends moral weight to the novel's chilling attack on the town's salaried and propertied citizens, enabling Dorn to conclude that despite enormous losses at the margins of American society, "the world's even more distasteful from the other side" (102).

This process of cultural accounting reaches its highest level of generalization in "The Tunnel." The chapter considers the industrial organization of labor and argues that management's "planned policy to sequester men from work they are on the one hand forced to do, is one of the primary aims of the modern state: it is a planned murder beside which war is of little consequence." Dorn does not, however, allow either himself or his audience to rest secure in this self-righteous fury, instead disrupting complacency by immediately adding: "But in a world in which populations grow much faster than real work, such disclosures become pointless" (177). If this seems unduly cynical, it is nonetheless persuasive within the framework of *By the Sound* and exemplifies Dorn's unrelentingly negative vision of the West as emblem of America's failed promise.

The Shoshoneans (1966) extends this anatomy of the West into documentary non-fiction. Produced in collaboration with the black photographer Leroy Lucas, this is a hybrid work. Dorn's mixture of historical research, ecological analysis, personal narrative, and sociological speculation envelops Lucas's stark images of the Paiutes, Western Shoshones, and Bannocks who inhabit the Basin-Plateau region of Idaho and Nevada. Like "The Land Below" and "Idaho

Out," *The Shoshoneans* loosely structures itself about a journey: in this instance, a field trip Dorn and Lucas took in the summer of 1965 that began in Reno, stretched through Duck Valley, and ended at the Fort Hall reservation near Pocatello. This geographical route also defines the book's thematic trajectory, which moves from "the psycho-peripheral sickness" (71) of Reno's urban Indians to the curative ritual of the revived Sun Dance at Fort Hall. Between these extremes of total deracination from the past and self-conscious recuperation of ancient roots stand what Dorn labels the "progressives," those Indians that seek assimilation into the white society and are most prominent on economically viable reservations like Duck Valley.

Dorn offers equivocal sympathy to each of these groups, intellectually endorsing the traditionalists' efforts to preserve Indian customs, emotionally identifying with "deculturized" Indians whose lives are marked by an uncluttered futility that parallels his own alienation, and even encouraging compassion for the "White Indians" whose desire for social integration he regards as self-destructive. But *The Shoshoneans* shows no indulgence in its clinical scrutiny of the dominant white culture. Dorn understands the contemporary "neo-wild West" (28) as a world controlled by "the innate, dynamic fascism" of "the nineteenth- and twentieth-century cowboy character" (31). The frontier's legendary fast draws and lynchings have become today's local police, meanly intolerant of strangers and alert for "*any* irregularity . . . not simply the obvious signals—untrimmed hair, a beard, poor shoes, an old coat" (34). Indeed, the nation's "whole citizenry" is now "a constabulary . . . one vast huge policeman," Dorn observes in "The Poet, the People, the Spirit," a lecture that also rehearses his and Lucas's trip (*Views* 93-117).

Motivated by paranoid fear of "dark, unAmerican forces," the country is possessed by a deep urge to destroy cultural difference.

This manifests itself domestically—*The Shoshoneans* argues—in the racist massacres at Wounded Knee (1890) and in Watts (1965) and globally in imperialist wars like Vietnam (45, 27). American democracy has thus become in practice a spiritually oppressive "homogeny" that demands in exchange for its economic benefits mindless allegiance to "the cheap and dishonorable mentalism of the 'American Dream'" (85-6). And for Dorn its ideal embodiment is Nevada, that "corny, flashing interzone" of a "no man's land . . . contrived to satisfy all specialty" of human desire without the inconveniences of reality. Like the country it images, Nevada is "No Where," so perfectly nonexistent that it is even "doubtful anything can die" there (29).

Cutting across the surface of this image of America's stifling emptiness are, however, signs of transcendence, disruptive moments in the text that intimate a contrary disposition to experience. *The Shoshoneans* opens with the most extraordinary of these gestures, Dorn's encounter with Willie Dorsey, a 102-year-old Shoshone, and his equally aged wife. These two so completely embody the tribe's ancient ways that their life has become a "full rite" that "reconstitutes the entirety of creation, the *Every Thing*." Though upset by the heat and filth of their tiny house and disturbed by the couple's acute physical decrepitude, Dorn is nonetheless overwhelmed by the intensity of their presence. Manifesting "the spirit that lies at the bottom, where we have our feet," this man and woman are for Dorn "the most profoundly beautiful ancestors I've witnessed" (12-13). Similar hints of a reality that transcends the limits of American culture occur in the mesmerizing impact of culturalist Willie George's voice (77-78) and in the "subtle clarity and calm" that permeates Lucas after his participation in the Sun Dance (79).

But in all of these instances, Dorn remains personally outside the events he describes, scrupulously respecting their difference from himself. This refusal to translate the unfamiliar into the language of his own sensibility is a profoundly revolutionary gesture. For Dorn is, in effect, denying the imperial habit of the American mind, which subjugates the foreign by assimilating its essential otherness into its own rationality. Nowhere is his rejection of America's colonizing consciousness clearer than at the end of *The Shoshoneans*. Instead of exercising the artist's privilege to bring his subject under final control by completing the imposition of aesthetic form, Dorn reserves his book's last five pages for a speech by an Indian activist, Clyde Warrior. This deferral to another's voice is a political act that acknowledges his subject's right to self-representation independent of the writer's authority, and it reveals the distance that separates Dorn's art from traditional aesthetics. For he is less concerned to achieve formal beauty than to free his readers from the "modern method of the unregenerate living dead" which is "to shut the eyes" to "the weight and leverages of reality" (81). Because literary conventions often encode this politics of suppression, Dorn deliberately violates them in order to liberate his audience's attention. This truly democratic project assumes greater momentum and sophistication in the next phase of his career.

The Period of *Slinger:* 1967-1974

The North Atlantic Turbine (1967) ends with "The Sundering U.P. Tracks" (*CP* 231-32), a piece which looks back to the circumstances of *The Shoshoneans* at the same time that it completes this new collection's title poem. Its occasion is Lucas' arrival in Pocatello and its theme Dorn's shocked recognition of the class and racial divisions inflicted on the West by "rapacious geo-economic" forces here represented by the Union Pacific's railroad tracks, that "shining double knife" which gashes the landscape from Chicago to Oregon. The poem's subtitle also indicates that it forms a coda to "The

North Atlantic Turbine" (*CP* 179-95), the difficult five-part suite which opens the volume. Though Dorn has criticized this long poem as "overreached" (*Interviews* 24), it remains important, since it demonstrates conceptual and stylistic developments that prepare the ground for *Slinger*.

The intellectual significance of "The North Atlantic Turbine" lies in Dorn's shift of focus from specific instances of exploitation to their underlying logic. The poem reconfigures the destruction of the American West by subordinating the trauma of individual events to the general advance of Western civilization's military and commercial might. In Dorn's argument, the Roman conquest of Britain foreshadowed the American intervention in Vietnam, just as the Medicis' banking empire in Renaissance Florence prefigured New York's Wall Street—all are links in an imperialist chain that is destined to encircle the globe. The machine that generates the power for this expansion is now centered geographically in the North Atlantic, and the poem enacts its world-encompassing triumph. Beginning with a haunting elegy for the remote Mackenzie Delta Eskimos whose culture has already been extinguished by white man's greed, the poem finishes with a farcical vision of the "End-of-China," wrought by an invasion of automobiles and "underarm spray deodorant."

This dramatic change in tone from the opening tragic note to the concluding comedy occurs after Dorn has carefully enumerated "a list of property to be blown apart / along the North Atlantic perimeter" in order to halt the turbine's progress. The list's fourth and last entry succeeds, however, only in highlighting the hopelessly self-defeating nature of this revolutionary enterprise. It announces, "Finally, the earth as primary object / must be destroyed." This prospect causes the poem to veer suddenly away from its moral outrage into a fantastic burlesque constructed around the public images of J. P. Getty and Hugh Hefner, both popular figures of American capitalist success. Dorn's ironic immersion here in the dominant culture's language and mythology marks a major stylistic turn. For it not only admits the futility of the direct polemical assault he has practiced earlier, but it also declares his commitment to a different tactic—comic subversion from within the society's own apparatus of control. Such guerrilla warfare becomes the fundamental strategy of *Slinger*, which summarizes the basic premise of the new approach: "Entrapment is this society's / Sole activity," the poem explains, "and Only laughter / can blow it to rags" (*S* 155).

Slinger, whose crazy-quilt texture is fabricated from patches of celluloid Westerns, country and rock music, comic books, mass media reports of contemporary events, and the jargons of numerous American subcultures, is a complex, multi-faceted work that defies easy explanation. The poem is already the subject of a significant body of critical commentary that suggests a variety of different interpretations. But for purposes of introduction, perhaps the most useful perspective is to view *Slinger* as a counter-epic of Western culture. The epic, whether originating like the *Iliad* and *Odyssey* in oral performances for preliterate audiences or produced like *The Aeneid* and *Paradise Lost* as written texts for educated readers, has traditionally been a repository of the civilization's values, an encyclopedia of shared customs and common wisdom that preserves and communicates the information necessary for social identity and generational continuity. The related mock epic, which *Slinger* superficially resembles, appropriates the epic's paraphernalia to satirize particular aspects of the dominant culture. Typical is *The Rape of the Lock*, which uses the mock epic's deflating laughter to correct excesses and restore social order. While *Slinger* follows this genre in ironically deploying the epic's elevated languages and formal conventions, Dorn's purpose is not therapeutic but lethal. His intent is an anti-epic aimed at destroying the very foundations of the imprisoning society.

This campaign is especially evident at the narrative level of plot and character. Book I deliberately invokes two archetypal formats of Western consciousness: the eschatological conflict between good and evil and the holy pilgrimage. The heroic center of both these scenarios is Slinger, a charismatic, superhuman gunslinger whose character wryly mixes Hollywood Westerns with the imagery of Christology. Identifying himself early in the poem as the 2,000-year-old "son of the sun" (15), he is presented as an embodiment of cosmic harmony and celestial wisdom whose mission is to confront his metaphysical opposite, that "inscrutable Texan," Howard Hughes.

For Dorn, Hughes is a postindustrial "extension of the earlier, non-electronic, financial geniuses like Fisk and Gould," a metaphor, in other words, for late American capitalism which dominates the nation's public life (*Interviews* 51). Like his historical counterpart, the Hughes of *Slinger* has come to abhor publicity and appears only in disguises under the names Robart—a near duplication of Hughes' actual middle name, Robard—and an off-rhyming alternate, Rupert. The "Cycle of Acquisition," Hughes' apparatus of social control, is the theme of an interlude between Books II and III (89-110). This transitional section also recounts Hughes' departure from Boston to Las Vegas in his private railway car, whose tracks across the country again serve Dorn as an emblem for economic tyranny. In Book III Hughes changes his itinerary in order to ambush Slinger at Four Corners, that point of perfect perpendicularity where the borders of New Mexico, Colorado, Utah, and Arizona intersect.

The events occuring early in Book IIII prepare the way for this climactic encounter. "The Hill of Beans," a giant bronze contraption located outside Cortez, Colorado, but "Hecho en Tejas / para El Hughes Tool Co.," is introduced as the John the Baptist-like spokesman for "Sllab," a code consisting of Chamber of Commerce clichés and computer jargon that is the gospel of Hughes' America (163-65). Dorn describes Sllab and its arrival on earth at greater length in a separately published, single-issue tabloid, *Bean News* (1972). Projecting a condition of "total Nothing . . . greater than the Void," Hughes' testament of electronic commercialism first appeared at Four Corners. Dorn regards this "giant plus sign" as "post-european man's greatest abstraction" and further explains that it has "recently gained notoriety for attracting the most negative aspects of western industry" (*Bean News* 8). Four Corners is Sllab's sacred ground, and hence the symbolically appropriate scene for Slinger's apocalyptic encounter.

And on this site there already rages in Book IIII a battle between the "new machinist" Mogollones, octane-breathing automatons that express technology's violent destructiveness, and the Single Spacers, sub-human survivors from an earlier stage of evolution whose anarchic energy opposes all progress. This war between the tools of capitalist expansion and the forces of nature would seem to prefigure the prospective clash between Slinger and Hughes, but in fact both sides are carefully controlled agents in Hughes' "Shortage Industry" (150), and their conflict is a meaningless spectacle with "all the hysteria of a fake disaster set" (194).

The bathos of complete non-event also informs *Slinger*'s conclusion, for when Hughes does finally materialize at Four Corners, he decoaches without encountering Slinger and abruptly heads for South America in search of new frontiers for his multi-national empire. Slinger himself is indifferent to Hughes' sudden departure and proceeds to close the poem with a set of formal blessings that are reminiscent of Prospero's conclusion to *The Tempest*. But

Slinger's benedictions, unlike Shakespeare's, mark no resolution. Rather, Dorn's art—by allowing the binary poles of his plot to drift aimlessly away from each other—disrupts the dialectical rhythm of Western thought and thereby voids the very premise that endows ideological conflict with meaning.

The paradigm of the holy pilgrimage similarly collapses in Book IIII. This teleological journey toward a source of value that will validate both self and society is as basic to rationalistic psychology as the epic battle between good and evil, for it ultimately asserts man's ability to define himself through exertion of his own will. In Book I Slinger assembles his company in Mesilla with the avowed spiritual purpose of learning truly "To See / The Universe" (46). The geographical object of their millennial quest is Las Vegas, which the group knows to be Hughes' territory: *"they say he moved to Vegas,"* one of Slinger's companions remarks, *"or* bought Vegas *and / moved it"* (9). The party's course toward the city is carefully charted, first north along the Rio Grande Valley to Universal City (Dorn's name for the New Mexico town Truth or Consequences) and thence through Placitas and Madrid into Santa Fe, before entering Colorado in the Four Corners region. This sense of forward progress lends structure to *Slinger*'s otherwise randomly episodic manner, until Book IIII when Dorn completely dismantles it with the revelation that *"Vegas is a vast decoy,"* an empty simulacrum of the reality the group seeks (169). Dorn's move here suspends the Western mind's privileged assumption of purposive, linear movement toward a pre-conceived goal and thus strips the reader of yet another cherished prop for sustaining traditional illusions of cultural order.

Other figures and incidents also support *Slinger*'s sabotage of Western patterns of thought. Conspicuous in this regard is the fate of "I," the character whose name is actually the pronoun that designates the personal self. In Book I, "I" is prominently present as the rational, autonomous ego of Cartesian humanism. Challenging any statement that contradicts linear logic, he is the butt of jokes that demonstrate the folly of expecting "reason to Follow / as some future chain gang does / a well worn road" (16). He constantly interrupts the flow of experience by interpretation, seeking to arrest its flux in the fixed categories of abstract meaning. But within the entrepreneurial universe of contemporary America, "I" 's addiction to descriptive knowledge can be fatal, for "If you have a name," Slinger explains, you are like a labelled product in the marketplace and "can be sold" (32). And it is precisely the death that attends man's conversion into commodity that "I" suffers in Book II, where he is subsequently embalmed in LSD (58-59). Dorn comically recounts the effect of this hallucinogenic drug on "I" 's expired rationalism (159-61). This expansion of consciousness enables first "I" 's resurrection in Book II (66-7), then his service in Book III as messenger for the pre-logical philosopher, Parmenides, and finally his post-logical assault in Book IIII on "all known species of Cant," particularly those centering on the concept of "Individuality" (162) that he himself had previously exemplified.

Contributing as well to Dorn's dissolution of rational habits of thought is a set of characters, each of whom, like "I," is linked to a mind-bending drug popular in the 1960s counter-culture. Slinger's "Stoned Horse" smokes giant marijuana cigars called Tampico Bombers; he also takes his name from Claude Lévi-Strauss, the French structuralist whose famous studies of primitive society revealed the arbitrariness of European cultural values. Slinger's longtime companion, Lil, is a frontier dancehall madam associated with mescaline and cocaine. Kool Everything supplies the five-gallon cannister of LSD which is used to transform "I," while Taco Desoxin embodies the manic energy implicit in the brand of amphetamine inscribed in his name.

Throughout *Slinger* the madcap mentalities of these characters erupt in conversations that cut across the grain of reason, exposing the linguistic conventions and intellectual premises that normally organize and limit consciousness. Symptomatic is Claude's punning statement that the distance from Mesilla to Las Vegas is "across / two states of mind" (41), which denies the commonplace divorce of spirit from matter by wittily conflating mental and geographical space—or Taco's "Hi-grade lunatic information" (167-68), which so totally scrambles literal and figural meanings as to destroy realist claims for language's capacity to represent the world unambiguously.

Along this stylistic front opened by Dorn's guerrilla warfare against Western culture, the most important figure is the Poet, who enters the anti-epic in Book I, identified not with any subversive drug but with the power of song itself to disrupt mental routines. Beginning with an erotic lyric whose oxymoronic style displays desire's power to confound logic (39-40), the Poet recites songs in each of *Slinger*'s sections. These formal performances include Book II's aubade, "Cool Liquid Comes" (50-51), whose synesthetic language creates an unorthodox fusion of physical sensation with spiritual intuition, Book III's "Riding Through Mádrid," an unlyrical celebration of nature that prompts Slinger to remember that "the world soul / slumbers in matter" (129-130), and Book IIII's ballad of Cocaine Lil (172-77), which invokes native American myth to intimate an archaic sensibility contrary to the Western mind, while it also parodies the primitivism fashionable among liberal intellectuals in the 1960s.

All of the Poet's performances wreak havoc on grammar as well as literary decorum, wilfully violating traditional techniques for ordering perception and thought. Their common "mission," in Slinger's words, is "to encourage the Purity of the Head" (63), and this intent is especially evident in the two songs that are probably the most opaque to understanding. "The Cycle of Robart's Wallet" (87-110) ostensibly focuses on Hughes' departure from Boston's South Station in his "Wingèd Car," but the recitation's actual concerns are the structure and condition of language in contemporary America—both its syntactical encoding of basic assumptions about reality and its semantic colonization by the society's controlling economic interests. The Poet's purpose is both to demonstrate language's inflexibility and to combat its corruption into rigid grammatical and cultural formulas that enforce dominant cultural values. His method in this project is to violently displace words from their familiar functions. Personal pronouns are twisted into proper names, verbs function as nouns, directional terms like "front" and "rear" are reified into physical locations, dialectically dependent pairs like "in/out" and "up/down" are logically severed, and the jargons of mutually indifferent social groups collide senselessly against each other. This complex linguistic play culminates in the Poet's description of the interior of Hughes' railroad car (98-109), which paradoxically collapses Plato's dream of abstract, timeless forms into the self-consuming nothingness of *Paradise Lost's* image of Hell—the positive and negative poles of Western civilization merged, in short, into one nightmarish whole. The overall effect of "The Cycle" is not easily summarized but may perhaps best be understood as a verbal rendition of that complete evacuation of public reality which Jean Baudrillard has recently ascribed to late capitalism in his book, *Simulations* (1981; English trans. 1983).

Countering "The Cycle" is another difficult song, the brief "La Lejanía" (178). While in Hughes' oppressively verbalized and socialized universe, "The shades are drawn against / The organ of the Imagination" (101), here the Poet gestures outside Western culture and the prison house of its language toward a geological context larger and more ancient than man. The poem invokes the mythic "Holly Holia," the sacred ground of cosmological origin. But because the literary resources of educated discourses are so debased, the Poet's prayer must proceed indirectly, avoiding as much as possible standard syntax and diction. Dorn's strategy is to cast into parataxis highly technical vocabulary and then to further remove his words from *Slinger*'s normal channels of communication by translating them into Spanish. The awkward result fails utterly to deliver that harmonious beauty readers are accustomed to expect from moments of lyrical transcendence, but in its stubbornly anti-aesthetic manner, Dorn's song possesses a rare moral integrity.

Recent Work: 1974-

The historical realism of *Recollections of Gran Apachería* (1974) breaks sharply from *Slinger*'s fanciful inventiveness and inaugurates the current phase of Dorn's career. Though stylistically different, *Recollections* is a tactical complement to Dorn's anti-epic, for it matches the comedy of *Slinger*'s internal subversion of American society with the tragedy of the Apache's "continuous run / of external resistance" to "Whiteye policy" (33, 28). These two dimensions of Dorn's campaign are, in fact, artfully juxtaposed in the paperback issue of *Recollections*, which appeared in a comic book format that incongruously packaged Dorn's grim verse in Michael Myers' extravagant burlesque of an American tourist. Against a desert background, this cartoon character sits astride a gasoline-powered cow, enmeshed in the paraphernalia of leisured consumption. This is a Howard Hughes on vacation, Myers' drawing wittily projecting a contemporary version of that "habitual craziness" (29) which in the last quarter of the nineteenth century conquered Apachería and destroyed its people.

The unbridgable chasm that separates white from Apache culture is the thematic axis of *Recollections*. Differences between them are discursively presented in the group of poems running from "Reservations" (26-29) through "So" (37). The American "predictive Mind," alienated from the present and "waving pathologically at the future" (27, 37), is set implacably against the Apaches, wholly "devoted to pure observation" of the immediate world of nature and with "no mechanic of the future" (34, 37). In Dorn's argument, that marriage of "Native" and "Alien Thinking" (33), which Pocahontas has traditionally symbolized in the American imagination, is a sentimental hoax. For not only are "the Northern Europeans" who settled the continent unable "to live on Earth with other kinds" but also "Apache policy was to extirpate / Every trace of civilization" (26, 13).

Recollections begins by exploring this conflict through a series of historical portraits. These include individual images of the war chiefs Victorio, Geronimo, and Nanay, of a U.S. Cavalry officer, Emmet Crawford, and of a traitorous Apache scout, Peaches (11-23), and are like snapshots, transfixing their subjects in carefully considered poses. And indeed, the governing stylistic mode of *Recollections* is photography, which becomes explicit in the volume's concluding piece, "La Máquina a Houston" (42-44). This poem's occasion is the arrival in Houston of the railroad cars transporting the last remnants of Apache warriors into permanent exile. Its point of view is that of a photographer and the soldiers who force the prisoners to attention before his camera. Photography here clearly acts to assert political control over its subjects—just as Susan Sontag had explained in a widely heralded essay published just a year before *Recollections* in the 18 October 1973 number of the *New York Review of Books*. And Dorn compels his readers to participate in this act of transgression by rhetorically identifying them with its perpetrators. "We are with the man with the camera," the

poem insists and then rhythmically reiterates the inclusive pronoun—
"We motioned the way with our shotguns," "We are struck and
thrilled," and finally, "We are too far gone on thought, and its
rejections." Thus implicated in the criminal imperialism *Recollections of Gran Apachería* records, Dorn's audience not only suffers
the resurrection of forgotten guilt but also is forced to recognize
itself in Myers' satiric figure—whose battery of equipment significantly
includes flashbulb and camera.

Recollections' vengeful edge continues in the cynical wit of *Hello,
La Jolla* (1978) and *Yellow Lola* (1981), which direct their corrosive
satire against the fads and follies of contemporary America. The
contents of both volumes derive from notebooks Dorn kept during
the late 1970s to record occasional thoughts and personal reactions
to events. While Dorn himself fabricated *Hello, La Jolla*, carefully
refining its short, wisecracking poems from the notebooks' raw
materials, the pieces in *Yellow Lola* were selected and arranged
by his friend Tom Clark, with minimal intervention from Dorn.
Typically briefer, blunter, and often more biting than their counterparts in *Hello, La Jolla*, they represent a sub-strata of Dorn's
poetic mind and provide an interesting opportunity to study his
techniques of composition and revision.

Though aggressively tough and wilfully provocative, the verse in
these two books is the most accessible of all of Dorn's poetry.
Its underlying premise is stated succinctly in *Yellow Lola*: "the
common duty of the poet / in this era of massive dysfunction /
& generalized onslaught on alertness / is to maintain the plant"
(63), by which Dorn means the intellectual machinery necessary
for critical thought. This poem's title, "Night Watchman, look to
my flashlight," also defines the method of the two collections, in
which the poet appropriates to himself the guardian's role and
demands us to attend his bright light as it focuses narrowly on

one suspicious intruder after another. Popular culture and current events are the subjects of Dorn's intense interrogations, which expose the unexamined contradictions imbedded in the values and opinions that are routinely produced for American consumers by the nation's mass media.

"What Is This Thing Called Contemplation" (*Hello* 70-71) exemplifies the range and rhythm of much of this work. The poem opens by parodying the clichéd attitudes toward health, money, morality, and politics that typically furnish a middle class life. An ironic catalog of this pre-fabricated mental furniture is then given: "A fast present, a blank past / An immediate future / A wait-and-see administration," etc. The conclusion then curtly records the cost of all this verbal glibness: "An embarrassed language / in which Freedom / is thrown like a shrunk bedspread / over Liberty." This loss, in which language ceases to be an instrument for liberating consciousness but instead imprisons it in jargon, had also, of course, preoccupied Dorn in *Slinger*.

But *Slinger* addresses the problem essentially at the levels of syntax and semantics. Though other poems here, such as "Correct usages" (*Hello* 64-7) and "Super" (*Yellow Lola* 53), continue that grammatical attack, Dorn is now more often concerned with the larger packages in which the dominant culture processes and markets feeling or meaning. Christmas warmth (*Yellow Lola* 30), the virtues of a volunteer army (*Hello* 31), art's disinterested aesthetics (*Hello* 52, 80)—Dorn shows each of these to be manufactured commodities designed to short-circuit thought about social reality.

The cant of liberal politics in particular provokes Dorn's contempt, precisely because it encourages a "flourishing, abundant, moral conscientiousness" that disguises how "essentially dishonest & self-serving" are its causes. A "*collaboration* w/Satan" is, in fact, the indictment he returns against this pious rhetoric in the archly titled

"Suctorial" (*Yellow Lola* 44), and Dorn pursues this charge with malicious success in poems that bare the inconsistencies in the liberal position on air bags in automobiles (*Hello* 22), the neutron bomb (*Hello* 23), and violence on television (*Yellow Lola* 93).

The longest and least characteristic poem in these books is "Alaska: In Two Parts" (*Hello* 32-36), which laments Alaska's fate as just another stage in the great American "history of land grabs." The poem's length and geographical specificity recall, in fact, Dorn's earliest work, especially "The Land Below" and "Idaho Out." These qualities also suggest his latest work-in-progress, a poem on the High Plains that is projected on a scale comparable to that of *Slinger* but in a quite different manner. Precisely such continuity of theme mediated by radical changes in style typifies Dorn's entire career, and his new work promises to open yet another phase in his engagement of the American West.

Selected Bibliography

WORKS BY DORN

Poetry

The Newly Fallen. New York: Totem, 1961.
Hands Up! New York: Totem/Corinth, 1964.
From Gloucester Out. London: Matrix, 1964.
Geography. London: Fulcrum, 1965; rev. ed. London: Fulcrum, 1968.
The North Atlantic Turbine. London: Fulcrum, 1967.
Gunslinger, Book I; Gunslinger, Book II. Los Angeles: Black Sparrow, 1968-69.
Twenty-Four Love Songs. Buffalo: Frontier, 1970.
Songs: Set Two, A Short Count. West Newbury, MA: Frontier, 1970.
The Cycle. West Newbury, MA: Frontier, 1971.
Gunslinger, Book III. West Newbury, MA: Frontier, 1972.
Recollections of Gran Apachería. San Francisco: Turtle Island, 1974.
The Collected Poems 1956-1974. Bolinas, CA: Four Seasons Foundation, 1975.
Slinger. Berkeley: Wingbow, 1975.
Manchester Square. London: Permanent, 1975.
Hello, La Jolla. Berkeley: Wingbow, 1978.
Selected Poems. Ed. Donald Allen. Bolinas, CA: Gray Fox, 1978.
Yellow Lola, Formerly Titled Japanese Neon (Hello, La Jolla, Book II). Santa Barbara: Cadmus Editions, 1980.
Captain Jack's Chaps, or Houston/MLA. Madison: Black Mesa, 1983.

Prose

What I See in The Maximus Poems. Ventura, CA: Migrant, 1960.
The Rites of Passage. Buffalo: Frontier, 1965, rev. ed. issued as *By the Sound.* Mt. Vernon, WA: Frontier, 1971.
The Shoshoneans: The People of the Basin-Plateau. New York: Morrow, 1966.

Some Business Recently Transacted in the White World. West Newbury, MA: Frontier, 1971.
Bean News. San Francisco: Hermes Free P, 1972.
"Strumming Language." *Talking Poetics from Naropa Institute.* Vol. 1. Ed. Anne Waldman and Marilyn Webb. Boulder: Shambhala, 1978. 83-95.
Interviews. Ed. Donald Allen. Bolinas, CA: Four Seasons Foundation, 1980.
Views. Ed. Donald Allen. San Francisco: Four Seasons Foundation, 1980.

Translations (All in collaboration with Gordon Brotherson)
Our Word: Guerrilla Poems from Latin America. London: Cape Goliard; New York: Grossman, 1968.
Tree Between Two Walls, by José Emilio Pacheco. Los Angeles: Black Sparrow, 1969.
Selected Poems, by César Vallejo. Harmondsworth, Eng.: Penguin, 1976.
Images of the New World: The American Continent Portrayed in Native Texts. London: Thames and Hudson, 1979.

SELECTED BOOKS, ARTICLES, REVIEWS ABOUT DORN

Davidson, Michael. "Archeologist of Morning: Charles Olson, Edward Dorn, and Historical Method." *ELH* 47 (1980): 158-79.
Davie, Donald. "The Black Mountain Poets: Charles Olson and Edward Dorn." *The Survival of Poetry.* Ed. Martin Dodsworth. London: Faber, 1970. 216-34.
Lockwood, William J. "Ed Dorn's Mystique of the Real: His Poems for North America." *Contemporary Literature* 19 (1978): 58-79.
Paul, Sherman. *The Lost America of Love: Rereading Robert Creeley, Edward Dorn, and Robert Duncan.* Baton Rouge: Louisiana

State UP, 1981. Esp. 77-168.

Sturgeon, Tandy. "An Interview with Edward Dorn." *Contemporary Literature* 27.1 (1986): 1-16.

Wesling, Donald. "A Bibliography on Edward Dorn for America." *Parnassus* 5.2 (1977): 142-60.

⎯⎯⎯⎯⎯, ed. *Internal Resistances: The Poetry of Edward Dorn.* Berkeley: U of California P, 1985. Contains important essays on all of Dorn's major works.

Winkel, Martha G., and Jean W. Ross. "Dorn, Edward (Merton)." *Contemporary Authors.* Vols. 93-96. Detroit: Gale, 1980: 127-29. Contains an interview with Dorn.

811
M172e   77624
McPheron
Edward Dorn